Global

Unravelling the New Capitalism

Peter S Heslam

Director of the Capitalism Project,
London Institute for Contemporary Christianity

Tutor in Mission and Pastoral Studies, Ridley Hall, Cambridge

GROVE BOOKS LIMITED
RIDLEY HALL RD CAMBRIDGE CB3 9HU

Contents

1. Introduction 3
2. What is Globalization? 5
   - *Three Schools* 5
   - *Two Paradoxes* 6
   - *One Dominant Trait* 11
3. Towards a Christian Perspective 14
   - *Radicals* 14
   - *Conservatives* 16
   - *Applying the Christian Story* 17
4. Conclusion 25

Appendix 28

Notes 30

'He rules the world with truth and grace' (Isaac Watts)
To Ulrich Duchrow and Brian Griffiths, for their inspiration and friendship.

The Cover Illustration is by Peter Ashton

Copyright © Peter S Heslam 2002

First Impression April 2002
ISSN 1470-854X
ISBN 1 85174 495 9

Introduction

McDonalds in Moscow, Coca-Cola in Kazakhstan, a Swede managing the English football team and Baywatch everywhere. Globalization is the buzz-word of the moment.

It is on the lips of journalists, politicians, business people, academics, clerics and activists. But what does it mean?

The range of opinions is almost as vast as the phenomenon the term describes. Some therefore dismiss the debate as 'globalony,' claiming that 'globalization' is a vacuous term encompassing every social and cultural phenomenon but offering little insight into the contemporary human condition. Its prevalence, however, reflects a widespread perception that in every area of life from cultural to criminal, from financial to environmental, there is a broadening, deepening and speeding up of worldwide interconnectedness. The sense is of a world being recast, through the impact of economic and technological forces, into a shared social and economic space.

Never has this sense been stronger than following the attacks on the Pentagon and the World Trade Center in September 2001. As leading symbols of US military and economic might, this tragedy and its aftermath have served to intensify the divisions of opinion on globalization yet further. This division partly reflects an increase in the uncertainty and unpredictability that have characterized the post-Cold War era. The only substantial agreement is that this is a transitional period. Many of the values, assumptions and structures that once enjoyed broad acceptance have been set aside, but new ones have not yet fully emerged. The resulting situation is so full of paradox that it allows optimists and pessimists to vie with equal fervour.

> *In every area of life there is a broadening, deepening and speeding up of worldwide interconnectedness*

The most sanguine view is that there is nothing to worry about. The resilience of the global political-economic order is guaranteed both because of its powers of recuperation and because there are no alternatives.

Given the scale and scope of globalization, the diversity of opinion surrounding it, the uncertainty as to its direction and the paradoxes with which it is riddled, this booklet aims simply to outline some of its key features and suggest ways they can be assessed from a Christian perspective. The focus will be on the economic aspect. Coupled with the technological, this is the central aspect of globalization and the one in which the ethical and theological stakes are highest. This is due to the rise of the 'new capitalism' and its implications for the future of the planet and its people. Although largely a western phenomenon, the processes of globalization are unravelling it across the globe. In response, this booklet attempts to unravel aspects of the new capitalism by means of clarification and critique. This is not, of course, where a Christian response ends. Crucial to any robust engagement with globalization is a four-fold task: clarification, critique, the search for alternatives and suggestions for action.

A publication of this size cannot sensibly, however, aim to cover each of these four tasks. But what I will do is:

- examine globalization by looking at the range of secular assessments of it, exploring its paradoxes and themes;
- look at some Christian responses, and attempt to set the Christian 'grand story' alongside globalization to open up some new perspectives;
- suggest some practical directions for our response to this phenomenon.

What is Globalization?

Capitalism is at one and the same time the best thing that has ever happened to the human race, and the worst.

Frederic Jameson, *Postmodernism*, 1991

The nature of globalization means that trying to define it is like 'trying to nail a blancmange to the wall.'[1] Clarification is best achieved through description rather than definition. This chapter is therefore an attempt to describe globalization by means of three schools of opinion, two paradoxes and one dominant trait.[2]

Three Schools

Globalists argue that the emerging single global economy, transcending and integrating major economic regions, marks the beginnings of a radically new era. In this new borderless world, national governments are relegated to little more than bystanders to global capital flows. Influence over economic power and wealth is increasingly located in global finance and corporate capital, rather than in nation states. Thus the authority and legitimacy of the nation-state is being dramatically eroded, and politics is being reduced to economic management. As people become less constrained by the disciplines of the state and more by the global market place, the end of the welfare state and social democracy is fast approaching. In short, the current era signals the end of politics.[3]

Demythologizers deny the revolutionary character of globalization, insisting that similar processes of integration have occurred in the past. National governments, they point out, maintain the power to regulate international economic activity and are both the originators and sustainers of economic liberalization. Globalization is therefore a myth. Rather than integrating, the world's political-economic systems are breaking up into regional civilisational blocks with their own religious, cultural and ethnic rivalries. Accordingly, notions of 'footloose capital' and the 'global corporation' are misguided; capital flows are largely confined to advanced capitalist states and the operations of most multinational companies are not global in reach.[4]

Restructuralists argue that globalization is transforming and restructuring the economic and political power of nation-states. They reject both the globalists' rhetoric about the end of the nation-state and the demythologizers' claim that 'nothing much has changed.' Instead they assert that through a burgeoning of complex transnational networks, a new kind of sovereignty is displacing traditional patterns of statehood. Authority in society is becoming increasingly diffused among public and private agencies at local, national, regional and global levels. This does not, however, spell the end of the state. As governments are forced to look outwards to pursue cooperative strategies and construct international regulatory regimes, globalization encourages a more activist state. Globalization, they insist, is the chief driving force behind the rapid social, political and economic changes that are reshaping modern societies and world order. They emphasize that, although it is not an entirely new phenomenon, many of its contemporary features are unique, such as the near real-time communication facilitated by the revolution in electronic media.[5]

In making sense of these conflicting accounts of globalization, traditional political or ideological positions are of little value. The three schools do not neatly correspond to traditional ideological positions or worldviews. Socialist, liberal and conservative perspectives can be found amongst each of them. Globalists, for instance, include not only neo-liberals who welcome the triumph of individual autonomy and the market principle over state power, but also neo-Marxists for whom contemporary globalization represents oppressive global capitalism. Opinion amongst members of the same ideological groupings is often sharply divided, therefore, as to the benefits and dangers of globalization. Globalization is a process, or set of processes, riddled with paradox.

Two Paradoxes

1. Interconnectedness and Fragmentation

Globalization emerges from all three of the above accounts as a process of greater interconnectedness—even if such integration is more evident in certain regions than in others. What is generally overlooked by commentators, however, is that globalization also involves fragmentation. This paradox reflects two important factors that also contain the dynamic of paradox.

Globalization and localization. It is often argued that globalization is chiefly about the extension of western—principally American—power across the world. Some, indeed, reject the term globalization, insisting on Americanization as a more accurate term. This argument should not be dismissed too lightly. As the world's largest economic power, the US plays a key role in shaping globalization processes. The implication, however, is that the US is immune from the impact of globalization. The events of 11th September 2001 make it clear that globalization affects US society as much as social life elsewhere. Globalization cannot, in fact, be detached from local circumstances. Although it involves increasing physical mobility, its key cultural impact is the transformation of localities.

> An example of such transformation is the establishment in many towns and cities of new urban shopping centres featuring retail chains selling branded goods assembled from components or ingredients produced all over the world. Despite obvious advantages to the consumer, the restructuring of the local economy involved has often meant the loss of a good deal of what had previously been considered local, including small shops, post offices, high street banks, pubs, studios and workshops. But such changes form only part of the impact of globalization on local communities. Another aspect, which is often overlooked, is the way in which, amidst strong globalizing processes, cultural, national, ethnic and tribal loyalties—often religiously rooted—are undergoing a revival in the world at large. Globalization is not, therefore, merely about the loss of the local (whether perceived or real). It is also about the strengthening of the local and an increase in the global significance of local events and circumstances.

The paradox of interconnectedness and fragmentation is partly revealed, therefore, in the fact that globalization involves a process of localization.[6]

Globalization and (post)modernity. The same paradox also reflects the fact that globalization embodies both modernity's emphasis on universality and postmodernity's emphasis on plurality.[7] At the heart of the worldview of modernity lies a belief in the universal rule of reason that will replace ignorance and tradition with truth and objectivity. This is reflected in the way globalization is heralded as a benign worldwide process of interconnectedness and integration, facilitated through the extension of western culture.[8]

The irony of the present situation is that confidence in the quest for the universal co-exists with a growing scepticism about the validity of the quest. As a consequence, the universal is rapidly being replaced by the much less well-defined concept of the global. This concept, sometimes referred to as 'globality,' lacks a grand scheme based on deeply held convictions and high ideals. It is about people all over the world being able to eat the same kind of hamburgers, drink the same kind of soft drink, watch the same TV programmes and use the same software packages—not about them sharing common values. It thus reflects the scepticism towards 'metanarratives' (grand narratives that seek to explain reality) that characterizes postmodernity. The ascendant ideologies of capitalism and consumerism may seem exceptions to this trend. In their contemporary forms, however, they tend to appear as ideologies in denial. They are propounded as the only systems that work, and it is 'what works' (however narrowly defined) that is accorded special status in the postmodern worldview.

An important social consequence of this loss of metanarratives is not only cultural homogenization, but also, paradoxically, cultural fragmentation. The postmodern worldview, emboldened through the rise in consumerism and made eminently transportable through the revolution in electronic media, inevitably encourages the spread of individualism and the consequent atomization of society. This leads to the opposite of universalism—plurality. This is the acceptance, in theory at least, of all forms of belief and lifestyle as equally valid. The emergent 'pick-'n'-mix culture' is one in which local forms of religion, morality and culture are relativized and repackaged as consumer choices. An example is the use of spiritual and ethnic imagery by Nike and the Body Shop.[9]

Confidence in the quest for the universal co-exists with a growing scepticism in the validity of the quest

Globalization is therefore an expression both of modernity and of post-modernity. It is modern in its universalist pretensions, and postmodern in its fragmentation and pluralism. This highlights the limited value of 'definitions' of globalization. These almost invariably involve notions of interconnectedness and integration. While this is understandable, there is a danger that such terms are taken to represent an organic, holistic development. Though much benefit can be gained by the world being brought closer together, the cultural homogenization of globalization does not imply social cohesion. It often means the multiplication of worlds between which individuals can choose to inhabit, either simultaneously or consecutively. Fragmentation is the inevitable consequence of a process based on atomistic individualism. Such individualism, underpinned by a rationalist and functionalist view of the world, was heralded in modernity but is maintained in postmodernity.

2. Inclusion and Exclusion

Contrary to the impression given by some anti-globalization protesters, globalization is not bad news for all the world's poor. The erosion of boundaries prohibiting the free flow of money, technology and information has brought to some deprived areas of the world some significant improvements in living standards. Private capital flows to low income countries were six times greater in 2001 than in 1990, and foreign direct investment has brought some significant financial benefits, including rises in income, employment opportunities and technology transfer, and increased tax revenues to government.[10] So for many people on low-incomes, globalization bears the promise of being included amongst those who enjoy the benefits of the world economy.

But, contrary to the way globalization is presented by some of its advocates, this is not where the matter ends. Three key areas of the global economy contain ambiguities which demonstrate that globalization is about exclusion as well as inclusion—trade, finance and production.[11]

Trade

The liberalization of trade is a key aspect of globalization, opening up many low-income economies to international trade and its resulting economic benefits. But the distribution of gains is very uneven, not only between countries but within them.

- In high-income countries, increased trade with low-income countries tends to increase the earnings of higher-skilled workers, but the prospects of low-skilled workers are often curtailed. While the welfare state plays an important role in softening the impact of such change, the prospect of tax increases to fund it are inevitably resisted by employers in industries subject to global competition.

- Although markets may be global, regulation is largely national, causing friction between countries. The World Trade Organization (WTO), concerned primarily with trade liberalization, has so far failed to harmonize national regulatory regimes. Trade liberalization is thereby allowed to proceed on a selective basis, favouring the interests of high-income countries.

- The USA and EU's protection of their agricultural sectors (despite promoting 'free' trade) means that for every $1 rich countries give in aid, the poorest are denied $14 in lost agricultural exports. The 'special and differential treatment' towards the poor pledged in the WTO's objectives is far from becoming a practical reality.

Finance

Since the 1970s, worldwide capital flows have grown dramatically. For every dollar of real trade, $13 were exchanged in world financial markets in 1979, whereas this soared to $65 in 2002. Current levels of international financial transactions are indeed unprecedented, with daily turnover on foreign exchange markets measuring around $1.5 trillion. Although this means a sharp increase in capital flows to low-income countries, these flows are often channelled into speculative activity.[12] While such activity can be effective in terms of wealth creation, there are dangers in allowing the 'virtual' economy based on finance to dominate the 'real' economy based on trade and production. The financial crisis in East Asia in 1997 demonstrated this very clearly. It precipitated a sudden outflow of capital, turning showcase economies into problem cases and causing widespread social fall-out. The experience of inclusion had made many people rich, but the exclusion that followed the crisis impoverished many more.

Production

Transnational corporations (TNCs) are key players in the process of globalization. When it is difficult to maintain a competitive edge in their home country, they often relocate significant parts of the production process in low-income countries. This provides a powerful stimulus for the integration of national and local economies into global and regional production networks. It also allows TNCs, who are not as 'footloose' as is sometimes claimed, to make a significant contribution to economic growth in low-income countries and to play a key role in the diffusion of technical know-how. However, restrictions on TNC activity, including their ability to exit economies when it suits them, have been substantially reduced since the 1980s. In developing countries such business flight can have damaging social consequences. This points to a further problem, which TNCs are generally unwilling to admit. Although they are often subject to fierce global competition, they are also among its primary creators. Accounting for at least 20% of world production and 70% of world trade, their influence is often able to rival that of states, raising questions about their role in the development of democracy.

The paradoxes of interconnectedness–fragmentation and inclusion–exclusion conspire to produce a situation in which the world is being re-ordered into winners and losers. This is occurring *within* countries as well as between them, thus rendering talk of First and Third Worlds, or of North and South increasingly obsolete. Members of these 'worlds' live side by side in the world's major cities. Those able to access world markets and reap the benefits are able to join an increasingly interconnected global elite while the rest struggle on the margins. According to the World Bank, 2 billion people are not benefitting from globalization and 20% of the world's population have 80% of the world's wealth. As a result, the fragmentation stimulated by the individualism, eclecticism and consumerism of a postmodern culture dominated by electronic media is exacerbated by a widening gap between rich and poor.

> *Globalization is re-ordering the world into winners and losers*

The link between fragmentation and exclusion and the rise of religious extremism and international terrorism can only be mentioned in passing. The reach of the modern and postmodern worldviews, extended through the impact of globalization, has not weakened the influence of religion in non-Western societies as had been commonly anticipated in the West. They are, rather, having the opposite effect. Religion is strengthening its public role and is providing inspiration for resisting western universalism and plurality. As one Muslim scholar puts it: 'Religious fundamentalism in general, and Islamic fundamentalism in particular, are panic reactions to postmodern nihilism.'[13] Samuel Huntington provides a striking image of how such resistance can take violent form:

> *Religious fundamentalisms are panic reactions to postmodern nihilism*

> 'Somewhere in the Middle East a half-dozen young men could well be dressed in jeans, drinking Coke, listening to rap, and, between their bows to Mecca, putting together a bomb to blow up an American airliner.'[14]

One Dominant Trait

Globalization signals the emergence of a new kind of capitalism, different in significant ways from the one on which Karl Marx and Max Weber fashioned their accounts. It also differs from the more stable, managed forms of capitalism of the period immediately following the Second World War. The reasons for the change include the move from a production- to a consumption-orientated society in the West. This is reflected in the decline of class-based political ideologies and the rise of a new economic consensus based on a consumerist ethic and focused on the freedom of market forces to determine the organization of society. Traditional markets, it is argued, have to make room for contemporary ones, even if the former are deeply embedded in society and culture. Because the market mechanism is scientific and objective, it should be free to cross all social and cultural borders, regardless of short-term costs. This view accounts in part for the increasing independence of the financial sector from the constraints of other sectors, including trade and production. It also helps to account for the rationale behind the 'structural adjustment programmes' which have often been imposed on low-income countries with negative effect. The assumption is that if a low-income country genuinely desires material prosperity it must demonstrate its resolve by declaring that it is 'open for business' and that the free market is welcome within its borders.

Often referred to as neo-liberalism, the new capitalism has become, since the decline of the political left, so much the mindset of the West that many are prepared to agree with Margaret Thatcher's famous remark that 'there is no alternative.' Although it comes in various forms, the leading type insists that corporations are above all generators of shareholder profit and promotes the use of the market principle in areas of society previously considered free from the market's demands. Thus the domain once thought to be 'public,' including health and education, becomes increasingly 'private.' The kind of society that emerges not only *has* markets, but *is* a market. Thus 'the market' becomes, in the language of the new capitalism, a metaphor for the whole of life—an all-embracing worldview. When applied to the world as a whole, it finds expression in the promotion of a global market economy. As David Held puts it, neo-liberalism is 'the dominant form of globalization today.'[15]

Revealing its Roots

The mechanistic and utilitarian outlook of this market ideology reveals its roots in the Enlightenment. The market, governed by the laws of nature, functions like a machine ensuring economic stability or 'equilibrium.' Good capital return indicates the social desirability of a particular business enterprise or financial investment. Growth is measured in strictly mathematical terms, based on a functional, numerical approach to the economy. The irony, however, is that a key feature of the new capitalism is the increasing instability and unpredictability of the global economy. Thus the political economist John Gray, once a staunch advocate of neo-liberalism, writes of the emergence of the global economy as 'a decisive moment in the development of a late modern species of disordered, anarchic capitalism.' Such is new capitalism's tendency to anarchy, Gray claims, that governments have no way of knowing in advance how markets will react—they are 'flying blind.'[16] The financier George Soros portrays the emergent 'casino capitalism' with alarm. He argues that faith in the laws of nature expresses itself in an unquestioning belief in equilibrium and in what Ronald Reagan famously described as 'the magic of the marketplace.' Such faith sits uncomfortably, Soros claims, with the way global financial markets actually operate, which is characterized by volatility.[17] In the imagery used by some commentators, the new capitalism is like a massive articulated lorry, or 'juggernaut,' careering down a mountain pass out of control, leaving havoc and destruction in its wake.

A juggernaut, careering down a mountain out of control

In sum, globalization can best be understood as a set of transforming processes, driven primarily by economic and technological impulses but having an impact on virtually every sphere of life, including politics, culture, education, religion and the family. These processes generate networks of interaction that transcend the previous boundaries between these spheres. The intensification and institutionalization of global interconnectedness through new global and regional infrastructures of control and communication is unprecedented. As such, globalization marks a new era in human affairs. The paradoxes ensure that it is highly uneven in its embrace and impact; it excludes as well as includes, divides as well as unites. For some it means a shrinking world that is put at their fingertips. For others it means that opportunities and influence recede ever further into the distance.

Globalization marks a new era human affairs

Caught between global and local demands, national governments are redefining their role. As they do so, conflicting claims that 'the state is finished' and 'the state is as robust as ever' fail to do justice to the complexity of the current transformation of political power. Although the state retains many of its powers, such as the ability to raise taxes and engage in military action, the sheer scale on which economic power is exercised frequently escapes effective mechanisms of democratic control. Meanwhile, as the world continues to divide into winners and losers, globalization is becoming an increasingly controversial political, social, economic, ethical and religious issue. The debate is gathering momentum, with protagonists on both sides unwilling to admit to its paradoxes and ambiguities.

3

Towards a Christian Perspective

The optimist believes that we live in the best of all possible worlds, whereas the pessimist fears this is true.

Anon

Most literature on globalization takes an unashamedly secular, anthropocentric approach. Even the growing amount that is more earth-centred often maintains a mechanical, instrumentalist approach. But globalization is not a neutral or merely factual phenomenon. It is also a spiritual one. As became clear in the previous chapter, globalization is infused with beliefs, values and assumptions. So it is important that Christians seek to develop a perspective on it that is consonant with their faith. Jim Wallis writes: 'Economics is too important to be left to economists alone. It is high time to apply biblical theology to the crises of our global economy.'[18] As yet, however, there is little that has been written in this area. But there is a wealth of Christian reflection on the market economy, much of which is relevant to a critique of globalization. Globalization is heavily dependent on the neo-liberal commitment to the priority of the free market in the management of human affairs.

> *Economics is too important to be left to economists alone*

Not surprisingly, Christian opinion in this area is sharply divided. At one extreme is the radical response which challenges the church to oppose the *status quo* and become an exemplar of an alternative economy. At the other is the conservative response which appeals to Christian teaching to legitimize the market economy.

Radicals

These writers address the contemporary economy in a prophetic way, looking for radical change rather than piecemeal reform.[19] The new capitalism, accordingly, is rejected outright on the grounds of justice and equality. For Ulrich Duchrow, an eminent German professor of theology and a key representative of this school, the church's resistance to it is a matter of foundational belief (*status confessionis*). This is because the new capitalism regards the economy merely as a means of wealth accumulation on the part of those with capital. Hence its drive towards deregulation, which delivers vast riches for the few but poverty and death for the many. Global capitalism stands, therefore, at the same moral level as apartheid, nuclear warfare and the Holocaust. The use of Christian theology in support of it is therefore equivalent to heresy; it condones the exploitation of low-income countries and turns a blind eye to its 'global interconnected fascism.'[20] For theology to be truly biblical it has to take the actual lot of the poor as its starting point. Indeed, the truth can more readily be found in the silence of the victim than in those who are generally considered wise (1 Cor 1.20). Theology has a prophetic function and serves as a critique of ideology.

Theology has a prophetic function and serves as a critique of ideology

Much of the work of the radicals is thoroughly biblical and theological in aim and orientation. They insist that the global economy demands an equally comprehensive biblical and theological response that goes beyond the narrow confines of Christian social ethics and integrates doctrine with action. Duchrow therefore pays particular attention to developments in ancient Israel, subjecting them to stringent sociological analysis. This is important, he argues, in order to avoid arguments that are theologically abstract or limited to individual spirituality. His approach can be regarded, therefore, as radical in the true sense of the word—a concern with the roots of theology and economics and with addressing systemic issues. It is also intensely practical in application, seeking to motivate and inspire the church to take its social and economic responsibilities seriously. His work thereby represents, in the words of one of his critics, 'the most palpable and decisive Christian response to the market economy.'[21]

These powerful attributes do not, however, make the radical school immune from criticism. There is a tendency, for instance, to lay too much blame for material poverty at the feet of capitalism. Little attention is given to other factors, such as bad governance, corruption and the making of harmful cultural choices. The world tends to be divided into oppressors and the oppressed; there is scant recognition that, because of the reality of sin, there are no innocent parties.

Inadequate attention is also given to the question whether, because of human sinfulness, the ideal situation is realizable this side of eternity. Consequently, the extent to which economic decision-making is bound to remain the art of the possible is not fully explored. It is also debatable whether a phenomenon as complex and multi-dimensional as global capitalism can be judged so unequivocally as to make its repudiation a matter of foundational Christian belief. Given the benefits of economic globalization, it is difficult to see how global capitalism can be considered on the same terms as the apartheid or Nazi regimes.

Conservatives

This school is strongest in the United States, where it is often referred to as 'neo-Conservative.' In Britain it is Brian Griffiths, the leading banker, politician, academic economist and evangelical thinker who stands out as one of the school's most notable figures. A convert from socialism, he headed Margaret Thatcher's Policy Unit from 1985 to 1990 when she was Prime Minister.

For Griffiths, the market economy is the best, most efficient, and least harmful way to achieve the creation of wealth. He bases his case on Scripture, from which he deduces such principles as the imperative of wealth creation and the necessity of private property. But he is keen to distance himself from the determinist capitalism of libertarians like Friedrich Hayek and Milton Friedman. Indeed, his concern is to rescue the market economy from the destructive impact of such ideology and to see it Christianized through the application of biblical principles.

Griffiths accepts that the poverty of developing countries presents the most formidable challenge to the market economy. Nevertheless, he is clear that the problem is the poverty itself, not the inequality between rich and poor. He rejects, moreover, the notion that global poverty is caused primarily through the exploitation of poor countries by rich ones, and that poverty is a problem for governments to resolve, rather than individuals. For him, global poverty is caused significantly by cultural restraints on economic modernization and by unstable and corrupt governments. There is no alternative to the market economy. As the only system that can secure the creation of wealth, it is the answer to global poverty.[22]

As the only system that can secure the creation of wealth, the market economy is the answer to global poverty

Although Griffiths lacks the sense of urgency and life-and-death struggle characteristic of the radicals, he shares with Duchrow the commitment to work out a political economy based on the Hebrew Scriptures. The question is whether his advocacy of the free market within a post-Christian society leads to precisely the opposite of what he intends; the more the reach of the market is expanded, the more 'secular' it becomes. Griffiths' solution is the revival of Christian social values through Christian evangelism and renewal. The problem with this, however, is that it makes his defence of market capitalism too dependent on such a revival.[23]

Griffiths' rejection of Hayek and Friedman's view of 'economic man' as a rational isolated individual can only be welcomed from a Christian perspective. It is hard to see, however, how his promotion of competition and the deregulation of financial markets can in practice avoid the rational individualism he claims to reject. Griffiths seems impervious to such critique. He insists that the market economy promotes not only strong individuals but also strong communities. This is because the corporation has become an important standard bearer of values in society, thereby fulfilling the role assumed by the family and the church before their demise.[24]

Consistent with his belief in the corporation as the repository of values in society, Griffiths is unperturbed by the dominance of the market over areas of life outside the business sphere. The question here is how compatible is this attitude with his support for 'mediating structures' that exist between the individual and the state, such as the family, the church, the school, the voluntary organization and the corporation. Surely mediating structures become meaningless and ineffective if one of them—in this case the corporation—is allowed to dominate the others. For Anthony Giddens:

> Devotion to the free market on the one hand, and to the traditional family and nation on the other, is self-contradictory…Nothing is more dissolving of tradition than the 'permanent revolution' of market forces. The dynamism of market societies undermines traditional structures of authority and fractures local communities.[25]

In the search for Christian insight on economic globalization, the work of Duchrow and of Griffiths offer valuable perspectives. While Duchrow's work is a reminder of the importance of a fundamental critique of the contemporary economy and one that looks for alternatives, Griffiths' is a reminder of the importance of looking for its reform on the basis of Christian principles. There is no reason why both projects cannot be considered valid; the quest for alternatives and reform are not mutually exclusive. The common commitment of Duchrow and Griffiths to the value of Scripture in addressing the economy stimulates a re-examination of the relevance of biblical themes that may help make up for some of the deficiencies in their accounts.

Applying the Christian Story

Earlier it was noted that an essential feature of contemporary postmodern culture is the loss of belief in grand stories that seek to explain reality. In the Bible, however, the reader is presented with stories of God and God's dealings with the world. Together they form a grand story, four main 'chapters' of which are creation, sin, redemption and consummation. The following is an attempt to suggest how these chapters apply to some of the key aspects of globalization, taking the variety of views on globalization into account.

Creation

'God saw all that he had made and it was very good' (Gen 1.31). That this description applies to the economic sphere as much as any other is confirmed by the economic task given to Adam and Eve. They are to 'have dominion' over the fish of the sea, and over the birds of the air, and over cattle, and over all wild animals on earth, and over every creeping thing that creeps upon the ground' (Gen 1.26). The terms 'have dominion,' 'subdue,' 'rule over' are often interpreted in an anthropocentric way. They are taken as licence to extract and manipulate the earth's resources in the interests of human 'needs.'[26] When Genesis 1 and 2 are taken together, however, it is clear that 'having dominion' is to be understood in terms of 'tilling' and 'keeping' (Gen 2.15), which are horticultural terms expressing nurture and care. The human vocation, therefore, is one of stewardship; human beings are guardians or trustees of the creation of which they are a part. As such, they are answerable to God, for whom creation ultimately exists. This takes us back to the original meaning of the term 'economics,' derived from the Greek *oikonomia*—the responsible and careful administration of the household (*oikos*) of creation for the good of all. Calvin expresses this notion in his insistence that markets are given by God as a means not of self-gratification but of service. This insight—that human beings are to care for God's creation for the sake of God's glory—provides the basis for a truly theocentric, ecological theology.

> *Oikonomia—the responsible and careful administration of the household of creation for the good of all*

It is also important to note that Genesis portrays human beings as made in God's image. This God, conveyed through Scripture as a whole, is a trinity of persons-in-relation. It follows from this that what is essential to human existence is being-in-relationship. In other words, human beings find their true identity in relationships, relationships characterized by intimacy and self-giving. This questions the way human beings are perceived in the process of economic globalization, which, as noted earlier, tends to be in terms of autonomous individuals. As such they are free from all obligation, serving their own self-interest. The competitive struggle for power, which is as much a characteristic of globalization as increasing cooperation, is an expression of this. The international economists who make up The Group of Lisbon have pointed out that competition is no longer seen as a means to an end but has acquired the status of 'a universal *credo*, an ideology.'[27]

The language of 'sacrifice' used about job losses is telling in this regard. Such 'sacrifices' have to be accepted for the better future of all—a future that is to be built on a yet higher degree of autonomy and competition. The values of autonomy and competition can be traced back to the beginnings of modernity, and find expression in the notions of 'the survival of the fittest' in evolutionary theory and of 'economic man' in classical and neo-classical economics. They have a dubious record, including monopolies of power, war, human degradation and environmental destruction. All this is a far cry from the human vocation to exercise responsible dominion towards the whole human and non-human created order.

A third insight offered by the creation story is the importance of limits. Not only were the first human beings forbidden to eat the fruit from the tree of the knowledge of good and evil (Gen 2.17; 3.1–3); they were also commanded not to work on the Sabbath because God rested from his work of creation on the seventh day (Ex 20.8–11). Yet the emphasis on 'growth' and 'choice,' which are defining characteristics of the globalization agenda, assumes that these are, or should be, unlimited. Within a world in which society and the environment are bound by irremovable limits, the unfettered pursuit of these objectives incurs a heavy human and environmental cost. A fuller appreciation of the creation story leads to an understanding of the economic as a means rather than an end. Holistic development becomes the aim. Trade, finance, investment and economic growth itself are regarded merely as instruments to achieve it. The flourishing of human and non-human life cannot be achieved simply by empowering individuals with new choices.

> *The flourishing of life cannot be achieved just by empowering individuals with new choices*

Sin

The biblical story takes a tragic turn when, rather than becoming obedient stewards in close communion with God, human beings give in to temptation and disobey God. As a consequence, human relationships and identity are marred. Markets, which are relational entities, cease to be vehicles of service and become an arena for selfish activity. Goods once held in trust become private possessions over which absolute and exclusive rights are claimed. Natural resources are no longer treated as 'commons' but are hoarded, squandered and abused, and thus become a cause of strife and violence. Deception, distortion and domination (rather than dominion) come to characterize the relationship of human beings towards each other and towards creation. Covetousness replaces contentment and becomes the basis of all human enterprise (Eccl 4.4). In sum, 'the effect of the fall was that the desire for growth became obsessive and idolatrous, the scale of growth became excessive for some at the expense of others, and the means for growth became filled with greed, exploitation and injustice.'[28]

The impact of this pathology is not restricted to the individual but extends to the whole of society. Economic structures that reward the rich and keep the poor in poverty are manifestations, therefore, of systemic and not just personal evil. In the prophetic denunciations of Jerusalem, the city as a whole is condemned for having a political and economic system that devours people like wolves and seizes their wealth (Ezek 22.23–27). Earlier in the same prophecy, Sodom, whose sins are generally associated exclusively with sexual impurity, is denounced in the following terms: 'She and her daughters were arrogant, overfed and unconcerned; they did not help the poor and the needy' (Ezek 16.49).

In the light of this, the defence of the 'free' market as the most effective mechanism for the distribution of goods and services has to be balanced by an insistence that markets are flawed. As human institutions affected by sin, they cannot be relied on to secure the common good. Instead, those who create wealth will tend to see themselves as owners rather than as stewards, or use their wealth to influence the economic, political and legal system to protect their own position. Thus the political sphere becomes subservient to the economic. The result is a situation familiar to the teacher of wisdom: 'the field of the poor may produce abundant food, but injustice sweeps it away' (Prov 13.23). Economic systems may thus become idolatrous, and so adversarial to God's norms of justice that they even become demonic: 'an institution becomes demonic when it abandons its divine vocation…for the pursuit of its own idolatrous goals.'[29]

The social impact of sin is cast in sharp relief in the story of the tower of Babel in Genesis 11. This story offers insight into some of the problematic aspects of globalization, particularly when contrasted with the story of Pentecost in Acts 2. The free market system is the *lingua franca* of globalization. It is the language of profit maximization, shareholder value, efficiency, competition and progress. As all can speak it, all can participate in constructing a new global business civilisation without limits or boundaries. Yet God's judgment fell on Babel's inhabitants for their conceit; their language became confused. The arrogant pursuit of interconnectedness ended in fragmentation. With the coming of the Holy Spirit at Pentecost, however, the divisions are overcome. People are able to understand each other again, not because they return to a common language but because they are enabled to speak the language of others.

People are able to understand each other again because they are enabled to speak the language of others

The question these stories pose, by way of analogy, is whether an economic system based on self-interest can deliver on its promise of unity, inclusion and unlimited growth. If not, there is a valid place for looking for alternative patterns of economic development that are more respectful of the natural diversity of the created order and seek to build unity on an acknowledgement of that diversity. The uniform language of the free market may not be as economically sound as it first appeared. There are other languages that need to be heard, and to be heard together, such as those of human dignity, the integrity of creation, justice and peace.

Redemption

The biblical story does not end in sin, idolatry and the demonic. The plot moves on to reveal that God in Christ is the redeemer of the cosmos. Redemption is not in the first place a theological concept but a financial one. A redeemer is someone who sets others free by making a payment. Without restricting its language and imagery of atonement to penal metaphors of redemption, the New Testament portrays Christ's death as the payment of the necessary 'ransom.' The impact of this payment is as great as the scope of creation and of sin. It encompasses everything: 'through him [Christ] God was pleased to reconcile all things, whether on earth or in heaven, by making peace through the blood of his cross' (Col 1.20). That includes the economic sphere as much as individuals; the *whole* of creation is groaning to be delivered from its bondage (Rom 8.19–23).

Redemption is not in the first place a theological concept but a financial one

Many commentators on globalization, particularly amongst the globalist and conservative schools, look to economic globalization not so much as a process in need of redemption but as a means of redemption—as the hope of the world. Regardless of all evidence to the contrary, the 'invisible hand' of the market will bring prosperity and liberty to all. But from a Christian perspective, it is only the cross and resurrection that can bring salvation. What is enticing about putting faith in advanced forms of technology and capitalism is that they appear to offer identity and security more immediately than a crucified Christ: 'the selling point of these gods is directness and security …they give us instant service.'[30]

Many commentators look at globalization as a means of redemption

Others more concerned with the harmful aspects of globalization put their confidence in 'corporate social responsibility' (CSR). This movement within the business community, which has gathered pace in recent years, seeks to place greater emphasis on the vocation of business to serve the common good. Thus it seeks to fulfil a key part of the vision of Adam Smith, the originator of the idea of the 'invisible hand' and often regarded as the father of modern capitalism. He wrote that the ultimate goal of business is not to make a profit but to increase general welfare.[31] The CSR movement is having a remarkable impact on the workings of business, encouraged not only by governments keen to avoid tax increases to pay for social and environmental welfare, but by growing pressure from consumers, shareholders, non-governmental organizations (NGOs) and churches. Much of it ought to be given an enthusiastic (though not uncritical) welcome as an attempt to put a 'human face' on the global economy. But CSR also runs the danger of being seen as an agent of salvation. As the corporate sector embraces the doctrines of 'ethical investment,' 'corporate citizenship,' 'stakeholder value' and 'sustainable development,' so the poor and the environment will be delivered from their plight. The movement has therefore attracted the charges of both naïve utopianism and 'global salvationism.'[32] However CSR is assessed, the redemption story opens up the possibility of the redirection of business: 'the downward spiral of the fall meets the radical possibility of redirection toward the kingdom in the cross and resurrection of Christ.'[33]

That story also opens up the possibility of liberation for those who suffer injustice and oppression from economic globalization. For Christ disarmed the powers and authorities, making a public spectacle of them (Col 2.20). That is why his message is good news to the poor and oppressed (Lk 4.18–21). If the cross is a symbol of humiliation, abandonment, suffering, powerlessness and death, the resurrection is the promise that these things have been overcome. The ransom to secure release from these things has been paid in full. The debt incurred through the sinful forces that are the cause of these things has been cancelled.

The debt incurred through the sinful forces that are the cause of these things has been cancelled

God's redemption of the people of Israel from slavery in Egypt is the archetype of this redemption. What is not always recognized, however, is that the background to this slavery was not invasion or colonization, but debt. In Genesis, all the people living in Egypt come to Joseph in the midst of severe famine, saying: 'there is nothing left...but our bodies and our land...Buy us and our land in exchange for food, and we with our land will be in bondage to Pharaoh' (Gen 47.18–19). This is the background to the stringent controls on debt, rates of interest, measures creditors may take in seeking repayment, and the length of time a debt can remain in force that can be found in the Hebrew Scriptures. The New Testament portrayal of Christ as redeemer is based, therefore, on the deep memories of a people who know how heavy a burden debt can be.

From this perspective, serious questions need to be asked of the way in which the contemporary global economy is becoming increasingly dependent on the dynamic of debt. Responsible lending can help the debtor create wealth and can thereby provide an escape from poverty, as many cases of foreign direct investment and micro-credit schemes illustrate. However, a loan can only be effective if the power of the creditor over the debtor is recognized and controlled. Economic globalization is characterized, in contrast, by the systematic loosening of financial controls, and a consequently staggering increase in international capital flows. In the face of Christ's liberation of humanity from indebtedness, it is ironic that people today are becoming increasingly willing to impose and incur significant amounts of debt and to tolerate what is rapidly becoming a debt-based economy, both nationally and globally.

Consummation

The final chapter of the biblical story is still to be written, although the Bible contains some lavish images as to what it will be like. It speaks of 'new heavens and a new earth' (Isa 65.17–25; Rev 21.1–5), in which there are no more tears, or death, or crying, or pain, nor is there famine or drought (Rev 7.16, 21.4). The glory and honour of the nations—presumably including all their cultural and economic goods—are brought into the new Jerusalem. There they are transformed, and no longer constitute a seduction away from the worship of God (Rev 21.24–27).

The question of to what extent this ideal state will be realized in history and to what extent it is an image of the life hereafter is much debated. Certainly there is much in current circumstances that would cast doubt on whether this vision could ever be realized in history. Nevertheless, hope for the transformation of current circumstances appears in the New Testament as an important part of Christian belief. In the Lord's Prayer, Jesus' followers are exhorted to pray for the coming of the kingdom of God *on earth* (Mt 6.10). Likewise, although the subjugation of 'the powers' under Christ's feet is a future event (1 Cor 15.24–25), it is also a present reality by virtue of the historical fact of the resurrection (Eph 1.19–23).

The paradox of the kingdom should act as a deterrent against both over optimism and doom and gloom

The paradox is that of the 'now' and the 'not yet' of God's kingdom. In Jesus' incarnation, ministry, death and resurrection, the kingdom has dawned and the promise is given that reality can be transformed in its light. However, although liberty has arrived for a world held in bondage, the full extent of that freedom has yet to be realized (Rom 8.18–25). The existence of this paradox, which lies at the heart of the Christian faith, partly explains why bringing a Christian perspective to bear on the paradoxical phenomenon of globalization is such a worthwhile and rewarding enterprise. The points of contact, whether critical or affirming, are immense. At the very least the paradox of the kingdom should act as a deterrent both against an overly optimistic faith in globalization's ability to spread the values of the kingdom and against the doom and gloom characterizing some of the more critical responses to globalization.

However well founded the claims of the optimists and pessimists might be on the evidence they cite, it must be acknowledged that there is an inevitable tension about the nature of reality in the present 'in between' times. The challenge in responding to globalization from a Christian perspective is to face up to that tension honestly and courageously, accepting the reality of sin and judgment but also affirming the hope of redemption. The impact of such a response can be profound. Faced with the ill effects of globalization, it will not shrink from prophetic critique but will point to hopeful signs of change and seek imaginatively for alternatives. Denunciation and protest, in other words, will be mixed with affirmation, hope, anticipation and celebration—as well as creative, holistic economic thought and action. It lies beyond the scope of this booklet to provide examples of how this can be realized in practice. In the Appendix, however, some of the initiatives in which the London Institute for Contemporary Christianity's Capitalism Project is involved are mentioned. These are attempts to respond imaginatively, within the constraints of a particular context, to the paradoxes of globalization from the perspective of the paradox of God's kingdom.

Our present-day relationships (including economic ones) are to anticipate God's better future

Just as the nature of human beings and the impact of both sin and redemption are to be understood in relational terms, the better future God offers in saving the world is a future of restored relationships. Insofar as God's salvation is a present reality as well as a future hope, our present-day relationships (including economic ones) are to anticipate that better future. The economic sphere, therefore, is not only good, fallen and redeemable; it is also able to point to the coming of the kingdom of God. Because creation has been redeemed, there is no place for fatalism, cynicism or complacency. Although all aspects of contemporary life mirror the effects of sin, Christ's redemption and the expectation of his return give hope. Hope that God is at work in the world and that the damaging aspects of globalization will be mollified. Every time Christians celebrate Holy Communion we anticipate the coming of God's kingdom—God's *oikonomia* of justice, peace and community. In the face of economic forces that exclude and fragment we celebrate and seek to live out Christ's inclusion and embrace.

Conclusion 4

The triumph of the free market, so confidently asserted by neo-liberals and echoed by 'third way' modernizers, appears to have been prematurely declared. The new capitalism is proving unable to deliver on its promises.

The widening gap between rich and poor and the continued degradation of the environment serve to make the limits of the new capitalism ever more apparent. Despite this, pressure is still growing on low-income countries to conform to the logic of the so-called free market and accept economic globalization as inevitable, even if it threatens their life and future.

The problems are rooted in a paradox. Economic globalization has helped to create better standards of living for hundreds of millions of people by means of technological and commercial growth. It also carries with it some of the greatest threats to the flourishing of creation. What has to be avoided in addressing it, therefore, is a blinkered approach which sees only part of the complex whole and constructs economic and moral arguments on that part alone. The full realities of the situation have to be taken into consideration, without fear that to do so would weaken a cherished position and give too much away to opponents. A rigorous appraisal of the full range of evidence, not just the narrowly economic, provides a way for the debate to move on. This must happen, for within a situation in which half the world's population live on less than two dollars a day, the need for fairer trade, biodiversity and respect for the environment has to take precedence over narrow political, economic or ideological concerns. Sustainable development cannot be dismissed as a novelty. It is an ancient conviction that goes back to the Garden of Eden. To pursue it requires the joined-up thinking involved in a holistic approach to creation that acknowledges its diversity. The interests of the environment, economic growth, security and democracy are diverse but also interconnected and therefore need to be treated together, rather than in isolation.

Sustainable development cannot be dismissed as a novelty

25

There are no good reasons why taking this range of interests seriously cannot be reconciled with concern for a buoyant economy. Neither are there any good theological or ethical reasons to resist the further development of the economic, scientific and technological potential of the created order—whether or not this development takes on world-wide dimensions—so long as the integrity and limits of creation are fully taken into account. The goal must be the well-being of the earth and all its inhabitants.

All this points to the importance of an integrated approach to globalization that recognizes its spiritual dimension grounded in both modern and postmodern worldviews. This has to be a starting point of any Christian critique, for it is the only way to ensure that the church's resistance to the ill-effects of globalization is theological and not just moral and ethical.

Mission in the Business Sector

To address the fundamentals of globalization in this way does not endanger the mission of the church in the business sector, as is often feared. Part of the reason why the church's voice is frequently ignored in business and economics is because that voice is heard either only to condemn or uncritically affirm. The account in John's gospel of Jesus' handling of the woman caught in adultery provides a model for the church in its interaction with the economic sphere. At the end of that account Jesus utters two remarkable phrases: 'neither do I condemn you' and 'go and sin no more.' The voice of the pastor is followed by the voice of the prophet. If the church's engagement with the global economy is to open up the possibility of practical change, it is vital that both these voices are clearly heard. To emphasize the one to the exclusion of the other will only alienate the spheres of church and business. It is unlikely that people will hear the prophetic voice if they do not hear the pastoral voice. Similarly, the pastoral voice is likely to be increasingly ignored as of little consequence if the prophetic voice keeps silent.

It is vital that the church's pastoral and prophetic voices are both clearly heard

The church can have every confidence in the relevance of its faith to this issue. The church is in essence—both theologically and practically—a global community. It serves a God who laid the foundations of the globe and sustains every area of life upon it. In Christ, God offers redemption to all its inhabitants and one day will gather all things together under him (Eph 1.10). The Christian God is therefore a global and globalizing God, and the same is true of the church.

Fighting Together

In fulfilling its mission, the church cannot, therefore, duck the ethical and practical issues, on the grounds that globalization is too complex, controversial or ephemeral a phenomenon. The Lambeth Conference of 1998 declared that since the previous conference ten years earlier, 'the greatest single new force shaping the world in which we do mission is the globalization of the market economy.'[34] In some ways, moreover, it is the church and its impulse towards mission that has helped to facilitate globalization. This gives it a particular responsibility to use all the resources at its disposal (both material and spiritual) to ensure that globalization works as a blessing and not as a curse to humanity. And we are not ill-placed to do this. It has been estimated that Christians control $10 trillion around the world—about a quarter of the world's annual production of wealth. If we were to decide to invest our wealth differently and shape institutions to achieve this goal, we could help to change the global economy.

Christians do not, however, fight this battle alone. By engaging in it they will find a host of allies, including many from other faiths. Increasing numbers of people in many parts of the world are becoming concerned about what is happening to the environment, the manipulation of their children by commercial forces—and their own lack of freedom and opportunity. The time may therefore be ripening for a re-orientation of globalization.

But this will only come about if change is effected on a number of fronts. Business and finance need to strengthen their social and environmental commitments; governments need to increase their resolve to meet existing targets in the fight against poverty and environmental degradation; individuals and households need to develop lifestyles that reject consumerism and exemplify an holistic approach to creation. Above all, there needs to be a willingness on the part of the rich to make room for the poor. Realistic solutions can only be found if an apparently unrealistic condition is met: that the lifestyle concerns of the wealthy are made subordinate to the survival concerns of those in poverty. The challenge is to handle the *resources of the earth* in such a way that the needs of the *people* of the earth are met without imperilling the future of both. Rich countries need to spread the benefits and shrink the burdens of their economies. Without self-restraint on the part of the rich, no serious long-term solutions or alternatives are possible. The power to withhold one's own claims may sit uncomfortably with the logic of the new capitalism, but it is the threshold that has to be crossed to lead the earth and its people out from an over-demanding global economy toward the realm of God's perfect justice.

> *Lifestyle concerns of the wealthy must be subordinate to the survival concerns of those in poverty*

Appendix

The Capitalism Project at LICC

The Capitalism Project at the London Institute for Contemporary Christianity (LICC) aims to develop a multi-disciplinary response to the theological, ethical, social and economic issues raised by globalization for business, governments, NGOs and individuals. It is involved not only in high-level teaching and research but also in developing resources for practitioners and non-specialists, including courses, study days and workshops.

The Project works in close association with a range of partners in business, finance, NGOs and churches. With organisations such as the Ridley Hall Foundation, the Jubilee Centre, the World Council of Churches and the Focolare Movement, it has run a number of conferences and seminars. It has also spearheaded the *Just Share* initiative, which involves a consortium of agencies, including Christian Aid and CAFOD, and seeks to explore issues of global economic justice around May Day. Together with Tearfund and World Vision it is working on issues facing development workers.

London Institute for Contemporary Christianity

Founded in 1982 by John Stott, LICC's role is to equip Christians to engage biblically and vigorously with the issues they face in the contemporary world and to provide resources and materials across a wide range of issues. Directed by Mark Greene, its particular focus is on work, capitalism, media, gender issues, youth culture, preaching and communication, and skills in engaging with culture. Details of its faculty, courses and resources are available on its website or by contacting:

> The London Institute for Contemporary Christianity
> St Peter's
> Vere Street
> London
> W1G 0DQ
> 020-7399-9555
> mail@licc.org.uk
> www.licc.org.uk

Grove Ethics Booklets

Grove booklets are fast-moving explorations of Christian life and ministry. They aim to be pioneering and innovative—not the last word, but often the first.

The Grove Ethics Series offers clear and concise explorations of contemporary ethical issues, including medical ethics, sexuality, business and legislation as well as exploring biblical ethical teaching. New titles are published quarterly every January, April, July and October and subscribers to the series save 15% by receiving new titles as they are published.

Grove publishes seven series of booklets:

- Biblical
- Ethics
- Evangelism
- Pastoral
- Renewal
- Spirituality
- Worship

For information about all our titles and to subscribe, visit our web site at www.grovebooks.co.uk.

To receive regular information about new titles as they are published, email news-add@grovebooks.co.uk.

Notes

1 Ulrich Beck, *What is Globalization?* (Cambridge: Polity, 2000) p 20.

2 In outlining the three schools I use different terms but follow the basic typology in *Global Transformations: Politics, Economics and Culture*, David Held et al (eds) (Cambridge: Polity Press, 1999) pp 2–10.

3 The political economists Noreena Hertz and George Monbiot are representatives of this school. See my interviews with them in *Third Way* (August 2001) pp 15–23.

4 A key text representing this school is Paul Hirst and Grahame Thompson, *Globalization in Question: The International Economy and the Possibilities of Governance* (Cambridge: Polity Press, 2nd edn, 1999).

5 An example of the re-structuralist perspective is Anthony Giddens, *The Consequences of Modernity* (Cambridge: Polity Press, 1990). The pace of the electonic revolution is reflected in the words of the former US President Bill Clinton in a recent lecture at the London School of Economics: 'When I became president in January 1993, there were only 50 sites on the World Wide Web. When I left office eight years later, there were 350 million.'

6 I am using the term 'localization' in the way it is often used by sociologists. See, for instance, Beck, *What is Globalization?* p45. The same term is also used to articulate an alternative vision to that of globalization such as that of Colin Hines, *Localization: A Global Manifesto* (London: Earthscan, 2000).

7 Sociologists disagree about the appropriateness of the term 'postmodernity,' many preferring 'late modernity.' The differences, however, are chiefly ones of emphasis regarding the degree of continuity with 'modernity.'

8 Many non-Westerners regard modernity as Western and imperialist rather than universal and benign. See Zygmunt Bauman, *Life in Fragments: Essays in Postmodern Moralities* (Oxford: Blackwell, 1995) p 24; Samuel P Huntington, *The Clash of Civilizations and the Remaking of World Order* (London: Touchstone Books, 1998), pp 55–7, 66.

9 Robert Goldman and Stephen Papson, *Nike Culture: The Sign of the Swoosh* (London: Sage, 1998) p 147; Ziauddin Sardar, *Postmodernism and the Other* (London: Pluto Press, 1998) pp 124–5.

10 See the World Bank reports at www.worldbank.org

11 I am particularly dependent on *Global Transformations* (see note 2 above) for the information contained in these summaries.

12 John Gray records that around 95% of transactions in foreign exchange markets are speculative in nature. John Gray, *False Dawn: The Delusions of Global Capitalism* (London: Granta Books, 1998) p 62.

13 Sardar, *Postmodernism and the Other*, p 244.

14 Huntington, *The Clash of Civilizations*, p 58.

15 'Globalization After 11 September: The Argument of Our Time,' a dialogue at www.opendemocracy.net between David Held and Paul Hirst. Held characterizes neo-liberalism with the phrases 'the impossibility of politics' and 'let the markets sort it out.'

16 Gray, pp 71, 62.

17 See Soros' *The Crisis of Global Capitalism: Open Society Endangered* (London: Little, Brown and Company, 1998) and his *Open Society: Reforming Global Capitalism* (London: Little, Brown and Company, 2000) pp 196–8.

18 From the *Sojourners* magazine. Cited in Ulrich Duchrow, *Alternatives to Global Capitalism, Drawn from Biblical History, Designed for Political Action* (Utrecht: International Books, 1995) p 1.

19 In this booklet the radical stream is taken to include the Latin American liberation theologians as well as the European theologians Ulrich Duchrow and Timothy Gorringe.

20 Ulrich Duchrow, *Global Economy: A Confessional Issue for the Churches?* (Geneva: WCC, 1987) p 115.

21 John Atherton, *Christianity and the Market: Christian Social Thought for Our Times* (London: SPCK, 1992) p 117.

22 Brian Griffiths, *Morality and the Market Place: Christian Alternatives to Capitalism and Socialism* (London: Hodder & Stoughton, 1982) pp 125, 143.

23 See Donald Hay, *Economics Today: A Christian Critique* (Leicester: Apollos, 1989) p 173. Hay questions whether Christian renewal would necessarily bring the desired effect, pointing out that 'the values of the secular market economy have taken deep roots in the Christian church, perhaps particularly the evangelical churches.'

24 Brian Griffiths, 'The Business Corporation as a Moral Community,' in *Capitalism, Morality and Markets*, edited by Brian Griffiths *et al* (London: The Institute of Economic Affairs, 2001) pp 17–40 (p 39); Brian Griffiths, 'The Culture of the Market,' in *Christianity and the Culture of Economics*, Donald A Hay and Alan Kreider (eds) (Wales: University of Wales Press, 2001) pp 12–32 (p 26).

25 Anthony Giddens, *The Third Way: The Renewal of Social Democracy* (Oxford:

Blackwell, 1998) p 15. Bishop Richard Harries echoes this point in 'The Third Way,' in *Crucible* (January–March 2001) pp 25–42 (p 33).

26 See, for instance, Griffiths, *Morality*, pp 79–80 and Richard Higginson, *Transforming Leadership: A Christian Approach to Management* (London: SPCK, 1996) p 7.

27 The Group of Lisbon, *Limits to Competition* (Cambridge, MA: MIT Press, 1995) p xii.

28 Christopher Wright, *Living as the People of God: The Relevance of Old Testament Ethics* (Leicester: IVP, 1983) p 81.

29 Walter Wink, *Engaging the Powers: Discernment and Resistance in a World of Domination* (Minneapolis, Minn: Fortress Press, 1992) p 72.

30 Kosuke Koyama, *Mt Fuji and Mt Sinai: A Critique of Idols* (Maryknoll, NY: Orbis Books, 1985) p 259.

31 Adam Smith, *The Wealth of Nations*, book 4, chapter 6. Despite his determinism, Smith makes moral demands, insisting that people sacrifice self-interest for the interest of the community (book 5, chapter 1, part 3).

32 David Henderson, *Misguided Virtue: False Notions of Corporate Social Responsibility* (London: Institute of Economic Affairs, 2001) pp 82–106.

33 Bryant L Myers, *Walking with the Poor: Principles and Practices of Transformational Development* (Maryknoll, NY: Orbis, 1999), p 36.

34 *Official Report of the Lambeth Conference 1998* (London: Morehouse, 1999) p 120.